STICKS

and

squiggles

Nonsense by
Janice Windle

To Sue
with best wishes —
Jan Windle.

Sticky Ends and Squiggles
(Nonsense by Janice Windle)
was first published in 2010 as a pamphlet
(ISBN: 978-1-907435-05-8)

www.dempseyandwindle.co.uk

This second edition
includes several additional poems.

ISBN: 978-1-907435-16-4

Other collections available from
www.dempseyandwindle.com and
www.lulu.com:

Sifting Sound into Shape by Dónall Dempsey

Dragged by the Cat Across the Carpet by Dónall Dempsey

Wordless Book by Dónall Dempsey

How to Make a Dress out of Silence by Janice Windle

Anti-Gravity by Janice Windle

Loving the Light by Janice Windle

CONTENTS

ONE OF THOSE DAYS

It was one of those days when without any warning
the space-time continuum shifted to morning –

the twin suns had risen, the nine moons had set
and the kitchen called, "Master, you want breakfast yet?"

I lay in my capsule, so snug and so lazy
but all of a sudden the vidscreens went crazy -

the newscaster rolled all his seventeen eyes
and said, "Monsters have landed from out of the skies!

They only have two legs to stand on, one head!"
I sat up in shock and I leapt out of bed -

it was one of those days when I had to go out
and meet those invaders my dream was about -

I tried to stay calm, but I'd had quite a fright -
I shouldn't read Philip K Dick late at night!

LOVE IN ICELAND

You kissed my ear
next to the breakfast cereals.
The snap. crackle, pop
of the gaze of the fat woman
pulling muesli off the shelf
deafened me, but you didn't care.

In the meat aisle,
you felt my rump
and pronounced it rare,
lean and probably tasty.

You expressed a wish to sample it
- later, I said, and hurried on
to the dairy products
 but cream was too erotic a concept
and hastily I steered us to
the frozen food department

which brought out the beast in you,
and you became a polar bear,
the cuddly smothery kind,
begging for Penguins
as we stood in the queue
in Iceland.

POP-UP

You gave me the Kama Sutra.
The pop-up edition - with full
chance for reader participation,
and plenty of tabs to pull.
There are pictures of bendy brown beauties
dressed in scanty but elegant clothes...
who show no resistance
to smiling insistence
by amorous Indian beaux.

You gave me the Kama Sutra
(pop-up version – it's so realistic)
The men all have cute little lingams
and there's tabs so the reader can swing them,
and the ladies are kissed,
not a square inch is missed,
from their yoni
right down to their wiggly toes.

You gave me the Kama Sutra
moving pictures to show what to do
and lots of advice
how to make love feel nice
and you popped up (like you always do.)

You gave me the Kama Sutra
and I know that we have a fine future;
the practice of loving
depends on the moving
of all body parts,
above all the heart,
and that's how I know that I suit ya!

DOMESTIC ARCHAEOLOGY

Two old pennies
stick of gum
fingerless glove
without a thumb
newspaper cutting
of Charles and Di
piece of toast
Jack's glass eye
rabbit's paw
plastic ring
unidentifiable... thing
furry thong
fluffy toy
card that says
that it's a boy
shopping list
from ninety-six
(don't forget
the Weetabix)
skeleton of
the guinea pig
lock of hair
from Grandma's wig
sweetie wrapper

Dad's false teeth
postcard sent
from Cowdenbeath
Grandpa's medals
the baby's dummy
pills for Auntie's
dicky tummy
sticky toffee
chicken feathers
bits of pizza
stuck together
down the back
of our settee – that's
domestic
archaeology.

THE UNFORTUNATE TALE OF JOHN

who would not do the ironing
but lived to cheer West Ham to victory.

John said that he was a "new man"-
That is, until his wife began
asking John to help her more -
he told her - "Listen, here's the score:
Housework is women's work," he said -
that's the reason I got wed –
ironing shirts when West Ham's on the telly?
Oh no, no way, not on your nelly!"

His wife, whose name was Susan, smiled -
"You said you'd help me – you beguiled
me when we met – now keep your word!"
but John pretends he hasn't heard.
and as her words fall on deaf ears,
and West Ham wins to Johnny's cheers,

she packs her bags and off she goes -
to meet an MCP she knows
who won't wash up –
 but is a lot more fun in bed than John

Moral:
A woman who is tired of ironing is tired of married life ...

THE ELEVATING STORY OF MISS X

who found True Love upon the Internet.

A quiet single girl, Miss X,
longed to meet the other sex
but being most extremely shy
she'd let her chances pass her by.

She registered with MeetAMate
posted her photo on the Net -
an old one – although pushing forty
she'd lied, "I'm twenty –five, and naughty!"

A date was planned, a meeting place -
the man looked at her aging face
and said, "I really have to leave -
My wife is sick!" – would you believe!

Miss X went home, she didn't care -
MARRIED! And such AWFUL hair!
Miss X rewrote her own description;
she told the truth, with no deception

and was besieged by handsome bucks
all in their twenties, wanting love
from a mature, maternal wife -
she chose the best, and CHANGED HER LIFE!

Moral: **Truth is sexier than fiction**

THE HEROIC TALE OF TRACEY

Who Longed for Fame at any Cost

Tracey longed for instant fame:
the public ought to know her name,
she thought - although she had no skills
or talents, she said she would kill
to see her name in neon lights
or on the news-stands every night.
She went on X-Factor, Big Brother;
friends voted for her, and her mother,
but stardom seemed to pass her by.

Our Tracey-girl was so insistent
she dressed in sexy tights and went
to see a very big producer
hoping that he would seduce her.

But Tracey's plans all went awry:
the man was rude, he made her cry:
he said, "No way! My casting couch
is not for such as you and – OUCH!"
for Tracey slapped his face, the brute,
and quickly she had time to shoot
a bullet through his grinning head:
the medics came and found him – dead!

So Tracey got the fame for which she pined.
They locked her up but she didn't mind.
She's written hit songs in her cell,
and her memoir's selling pretty well.

Moral: There's no such thing as bad publicity

The Story of Peter

who liked to dress up in women's clothing.

Peter liked to dress up in
His sister's clothes - not such a sin –
But when one fateful day he went
To work in mini dress and scent
His boss said, "Peter, there's a code;
Although you look quite á la mode
On the building site we're wondering
If cross-dressing is quite the thing."

At that our Pete was quite offended;
Gave notice, said that he intended
To go to court at the EU -
"My human right's infringed – I'll sue!"

He left the building trade behind,
Didn't sue – he changed his mind –
For soon he was a big success
Pole-dancing in a sparkly dress.

Moral:

Don't worry if you get a dressing-down for dressing up

MAN ON WALL

(after a painting by L.S .Lowry)

When Mr Brown turned up his toes
hung up his paperclips and rose
to that high office in the sky
his colleagues all exclaimed, "Oh my!
he makes a lovely corpse - a pity
not to share him with the City!"

They raised some cash to have him stuffed
(and Mrs. Brown said, "Fair enough!")
The taxidermist, quite a wag,
included Brown's habitual fag,
making him an installation,
a work of art, a fine creation,
and so he lies in splendid state
on the Embankment near the Tate.

HOW TO AVOID DIVORCE

I've been a true and faithful wife
to every husband that I've had
I've promised to devote my life
through thick and thin, through good and bad
but only while this rule applies:
what I decide shall be, shall be – and there
a problem lies.

When Johnny led me up the aisle
and with a manly loving smile
agreed that he would have and hold me
I loved him then but they never told me
I'd have to iron eight shirts a week
and when I ventured, "Could we speak
about this imposition on
my valuable time?" dear John
insisted this was what he'd meant
when opting for the sacrament.

As a blunt instrument the iron was great
John's status quickly changed to "late".

My second love was handsome Dave
Before we married he would rave
about the cute and charming way
I spent our weekends - how I lay
in bed, expecting cups of tea
and tasty meals to come to me.

One week past our honeymoon
I found that Dave had changed his tune -

"Get up," he said, "and get me bacon, eggs
and toast – come on, you do have legs".

I went downstairs and laid a tray –
I brought Dave's last meal up that day.
I even brought an appetizer –
grapefruit laced with fertilizer.
Sliced thinly, chopped and barbequed
he flushed quite neatly down the loo.

My third attempt at wedded bliss
began so well – we loved to kiss
and cuddle at all times of day
and let no chores get in our way
His name was Lee –a gorgeous man
but soon I noticed he began
to nag me to pick up my clothes
where I had dropped them – held his nose
and told me, "This house is disgusting –
don't you ever do the dusting?"
I got a broom and hit him hard -
he's buried out there, in the yard.

An optimist, I tried and tried -
again I made a blushing bride,
but number four is pushing daisies
gardening? The man was crazy!
and when it came to number five
his weakness showed up on a drive.
When I went through red traffic lights
he rudely said, "That wasn't right!"

While he checked underneath the bonnet
I found the accelerator, stepped on it
and drove him into paradise.
I know, I know, it wasn't nice!

So now I'm in an awful fix -
I need to find mate number six .

I think perhaps a poet will
be what I need, for would I kill
a man who sings and rhymes to me?
but one proviso – he should be

my greatest fan – he mustn't ever criticize my writing,
or my sharp pen between his eyes
will send him up to husband heaven –
and then I'll have to look for number seven.

FAIRY TALE

The princess sat in her father's court.

She was tall and fair and ready to wed.

She loved a man but her father said

the chap who'd marry his daughter ought

to fight a dragon, the fiery sort.

She wept for her lover might end up dead

if he tried to cut off a dragon's head,

because killing dragons is dangerous sport.

But she gave him a sword of the magic kind

and he galloped back with the flaming head

so the King had to order marriage wine

and the princess took her lover to bed.

(Some fathers try but can't, they find,

thwart daughters who have love in mind.)

THE PSYCHOLOGICAL MOMENT

A funny thing happened to me
on the way to this couch.
It was no joke though:
my Id decided to pick a quarrel
with my Ego and my Superego took sides.
War broke out within my boundaries
and my Libido became a refugee,
fled to a distant border
and left my anima behind to cope with
the decimation of its forces.
It was lucky that Intelligence
picked up Libido's whereabouts
and I found I was still Jung enough to know
the pleasures of losing my sang-Freud.

THE DISTRESSING STORY OF JANICE

who bought too many shoes
and came to a watery end.

This is the tale of Janice whose
fatal obsession was buying shoes:
a hundred pairs of shoes lay piled
within her wardrobe – her husband filed
for a divorce – he said the grounds
were: she was spending pounds and pounds
on sandals, slippers, high heels, pumps,
designer trainers, striped and spotty –
Janice bought them all, quite dotty.

Now Jan's obsession grew intense
and free from the good influence
of hubby, she went quite bananas,
went to Dolce and Gabana's -
no longer satisfied with Marks,
she bought with plastic and loans from sharks.

The outcome you'll have guessed, I'm sure:
her credit rating through the floor,
the loan sharks said, "Pay up or we
will give you *concrete* boots – you'll see!"
I'm sure that you will sympathise
with Jan's distress – she rolled her eyes,
and wept and screamed, went on her knees
and texted hubby, "Help me, please!"

Her grieving husband read her plea
but said, "No use to come to me!
You've run through all my money too –
I'm every bit as broke as you!"

And that is why, should you swim near
the Royal Pavilion, Brighton Pier,
you'll meet a little skeleton
with heavy concrete bootees on.

Moral:

You'll end up whaling if you deal with sharks!

THE STRANGE HISTORY OF HARRY

who Drove Too Fast and Disappeared from the Face of the Earth

Harry had a fault – the need
to get in cars and drive at speed.
He had no manners or decorum
behind the wheel – his worried Mum
said, "Harry you drive far too fast!"
but Harry thought it was a blast -
on motorways he'd always drive
at speeds exceeding ninety-five!

One day he passed a traffic cop
who waved him down – he didn't stop
and soon another five or six
had joined the chase; all Harry's tricks
to lose them, failed – but from the skies
before their unbelieving eyes
a spaceship beamed him from his car.

The aliens said, "So! Here you are!
We've watched you and our talent scouts
decided we should get you out
from slow old Earth! On our planet
slow driving's sinful and we ban it; -
Our cars are made of bendy plastic;
we don't allow pedestrians!" - "Fantastic!
Harry said, and went with them
To race his car on Alpha Ten
(His family were quite nonplussed
but no-one else was greatly fussed)

No moral here -

Harry didn't deserve this kind of luck;
He really was a dangerous ... driver

BETWEEN TWO STOOLS

You're not exactly a whore, he said, but
you're not exactly pure either.

You're not exactly ugly, he said, but
you're not exactly Helen of Troy

(he was an observant boy, this one)
and (he went on)

you're not exactly dowdy, but
you're not exactly stylish.

Your painting – it's
not exactly classical art but it's

not exactly *avant–garde*
(You finished? I said. I was breathing hard.)

No, he said, you're
not exactly Einstein but you're

not exactly thick. You're
not exactly analytical but you're

not exactly emotional,
he guessed...

Oh no? I thought. Yes, I said,
I suppose I fall

exactly between two stools.
And I picked one up and threw it

exactly

at his head .

YOU ARE OLD MRS. WINDLE

(after Lewis Carroll)

You are old, Mrs. Windle, the schoolchildren said,
and you really are not very cool.
And you look like you've only just got out of bed -
do you think that you should be in school?

In my youth, said the teacher, I was so hip,
picked flowers and did meditation.
Never took LSD – I preferred cups of tea
for my moments of spiritual elation.

You are old, Mrs. Windle, the schoolchildren said,
and you know that you can be a bore.
Yet you're trying to teach us and mess with our heads -
don't you think that it's making us sore?

In my youth, said the teacher, I listened in class
and tried to achieve the top mark.
But now I see clearly that I was an ass
so get lost and go play in the park!

THE SAD STORY OF MICHAEL

who was a Habitual Flirt

Michael was an awful Flirt;
his charm was legendary – it hurt
his steady girlfriend when she saw
the way he always hoped to score.

One night as Mike was chatting up
a girl called Anna whose bra cup
was thirty-two and double D
his girlfriend told him, "Don't you see,
if you go on, my plan is this –
I'll have to shoot you – I won't miss!"
But Michael said, "You won't you know -
you really love me, don't you know!"
And carried on to flirt some more.
His girlfriend, feeling very sore
like Cupid, took a bow and arrow,
aimed, shot - and his escape was narrow.

Her shot did not go through his heart,
But rather lower – it did smart!
and now his voice is quite high-pitched –
His girl's now seeing Anna –
"Bitch!" says Michael, "how was I
to know that both the girls were bi!"

Moral:

A bitch in the hand is worth two birds in each other's bushes!

THE UNUSUAL STORY OF MS JONES and her search for Freedom of Speech

Ms Jones was racist and a prig -
what's more, her mouth was very big –
she made a lot of people hate her
with comments of a personal nature.

One day when queuing up in Harrods
she passed loud comments on some Arabs.
Of course, they were upset and said,
"We'll place a fatwah on your head!"

Miss Jones was quite surprised – she balked
and said, "I am allowed to *talk*!"
An Arab who was called Ahmed
replied – "Oh no you're not," he said,
"and I suggest you find a man
as quickly as you ever can
who'll smother your big mouth with kisses,
turn you from M - S into Mrs,
and keep you in a harem where
you'll bitch and sulk and tear your hair
and turn your spite on other wives
who'll give it back with words like knives."

This lengthy speech turned Ms Jones red,
"How dare you!" angrily she said -
and yet she had to recognize
that Ahmed offered sage advice –
she flew straight to the Emirates
to find a polyandrous mate.

(The fatwah didn't work – although
assassins hunted high and low
Ms Jones was safe in the harem
of Prince Abu Nasir Naseem.)

Moral: Having a big mouth can take you places.

AS HE LIKES IT

On Spending an Exceedingly Long Time in Debenham's Lingerie Department Buying Bigger Underwear After the Usual Christmas Indulgence

I'm busy in the changing room
choosing bras, to fit my bigger,
well-fed, blooming, buxom figure,
buying lacy lingerie
to embrace the brave new me....

But this bra is far too small
and this corselet's too tight...
this one constricts, this one's too padded,
the shape – no it is just not right.
Assistance is at hand, I hear:
she tells me, "Try a fuller cup!" – Oh dear!
A double D! And it won't do up!
And I fear the added inches
call for pulleys and strong winches!

Dónall says my bigger bust
suits him fine, it's for the best,
says his ever rampant lust
is excited by my chest...

He's sitting by the dressing room door
I see he's writing, what is more,
and I wonder, as he snickers
there among the bras and knickers
is he writing about my quest
for underwear to fit my chest?

A WHOOSH WORKER

The brass plate beside the door read "Coaching in German, Japanese and Onomatopoeic". He stepped through the door into a bright reception hall.

"Can I oops there there?" said the pretty girl behind the desk.

"I see you are an Onomatopoeic speaker," he replied, picking up her dialect easily. "I'm looking for a refresher course in Onomatopoeic."

"Yes, sir, I am yakkyakkyakk in Onomatopoeic. How much ticktock would you pant pant to spend?"

"That depends on the chinkchink brrrnggg," he explained.

"We do a teenyweeny course or galumphing course, sir. If you want to lumber, take the galumphing course. The pace is less whoosh. When do you intend to visit Onomatopoeia?"

"I'm brrrrmbrrrrmming there next month."

"If I may yackety-yack so, sir, you do chatter Onomatopoeic very hooray already."

"I normally get very flutter-flutter when I speak to a fluent Onomatopoeian but your oooh hoorah makes me feel very aaahhh and mmmmm so I feel really yeahhh! talking to you. Would you pant to brrrrm out for a slurp and a chomp some tick-tock?" he continued.

She thought about this for a tick then said, "I'm quite a hush person but a whoosh slurp would be mmm." Privately she thought, "I hope he won't expect smackers and fumbling and slap-and-tickle afterwards."

"I'll bleep-bleep you" she said, "if you give me your ring-ring number." She clattered his booking and he clicked out of the door. In the brrrm-brrrm he felt very mmmmm that he had yeahhhed such a yummy Onomatopoeic girl. That night he snored aaahhhs of her sophisticated Onomatopoeic chatter and her ooh-la-la....

INTERNET DATING

You say you feel that we've already met… and yet

I haven't seen your face in truth –
after all, your photo on the Internet
may be a relic of your far-off youth

and

I cannot understand you
half as much
from your texting,
 as I would do from a touch
and if you tell me lies
I can't check it from your eyes
or the subtle movements
of a restless hand

and

is your B.O. a delight?
would I hurry from your sight
if you hadn't put some Brut on
as we sat upon my futon?

Over coffee in a café of my choice
would I find that I'm enamoured of your voice?
or would its grating tone
make me wish I was alone?

all these questions before meeting
face to face and so completing
our relationship – a test
that might not turn out for the best

for I fear that what is sauce
for the gander is of course

for the goose an equal trial
and perhaps you'd find me vile.

Virtual meeting of the minds
is a meeting of a kind
but to meet you face to face
even in a public place
would be very much more fun
but of course it can't be done ...

I suppose...

AMAZING GRACE AT THE SUPERMARKET

I knew it was an angel in the supermarket queue
by the feathers escaping from the collar of her beige coat
and the way the yellow hat framed her lined face
and the calm blue gaze of her crinkled eyes.

"So conventional, so predictable!" I thought savagely
and struck the angel's trolley hard with my own.
The angel turned, frowned
then rose, burst the buttons on her sensible coat,
released her powerful wings
and joined combat.

The security guard was looking away
as we soared, grappling
above the crowded aisles
up to the fluorescent lights.

I was smothered in soft down
under the strong pinions.
I struggled to grasp the wattled throat.
Breaking out through concrete
we flew together over the city roofs
and the angel's sturdy brogues

skimmed past my ear, en route for the stars.

Now the angel's feet were pink and bare,

her hat gone, bright hair flying about her face,

her forehead newly polished to an awesome beauty.

"OK, I admit it.

you WERE ahead of me in the queue,"

said the angel.

BAD RESOLUTIONS

On the last day of December
I decide that by November
I'll become a much more worthwhile citizen
but by March I'm always worse
so this year I'm going to try
reverse psychology.

Resolving that I won't be good
I hope to beat the stubborn mood
that's caused me not to keep my resolutions
about housework, punctuality
and with new terminology
I promise:

I'll stack the sink all day with dirty cups-
wash up? I'd rather not.
And why put them in the dishwasher?
Oh no – not me - I'm aware of
world ecology.

I'll iron shirts – but once a year's enough -
if you ask me to do more, I'll just say "Tough"
(I'll be too busy jotting down in rough
my masterwork on aspects
of epiphytology)

No cooking meals or making tea,
won't watch art programs on TV.
Instead I'll study something useful
like toxicology.

All night I'll sleep diagonally spread
selfishly across our double bed
snoring loud enough to waken up the dead
without apology.

I won't update my own website
with poems that I will not write,
I will not draw, nor paint – instead
each morning I'll relax in bed,
eat a hearty lunch, take forty winks again,
stay up late with chocolate and gin.
(Is that called Hedonology?)

And if I'm allowed up to a microphone
I'll drone on and on and on and on, immune
to audiences' boredom and the emcees' dirty looks -
I'll insist, I'll hog the mic and I'll plug my little books
forgetting to employ
reverse psychology.

CRUISING FOR A FALL

We booked a cruise last summer and set off for the Med,
"Ship ahoy me hearties," as Daddy bravely said.

Mum bought a smashing ball-dress to wear at the Captain's table.
She was sure that she'd impress because she looked like Betty Grable
(When Miss Grable was alive, of course).

We had to queue for breakfast, for dinner and for tea,
Never found the Captain's table and the vino wasn't free.

As we crossed the Bay of Biscay the waves grew very high
And we all leaned on the railings heaving up our chicken pie.

The weather growing hotter, Dad got places round the pool
(He said sorry for the fight he caused - he almost lost his cool)

Our cabins were below decks with very narrow bunks,
Not four-posters like the website - Dad said the ship was junk.

And he didn't mean Chinese, though we laughed about the pun
And we didn't mind the engines' noise and Mum was having fun.

But the stewards weren't all handsome
And the concerts were low-brow
And before we got to Naples,
The engines broke and now

We're limping back to Plymouth – the loos and food all stink
And next year we're going to book to go to Ilfracombe, I think.

MOTHER SAID

Mother said I should choose a man
with charm and wit and beautiful hands.
She'd lost a man like that and had
to put up with marrying my Dad.

I chose a man who was bald and fat
whose wit was blunt , who had no charm
and he wove a spell so that in his arms
I didn't notice he had no curls
I didn't see his broken nails
I thought he was a brilliant wit
I laughed at all his jokes and yet
when I took him home to meet my Mother
she said he won't do, go find another.

But I searched again for a man she'd approve
till I gave it up and went back to my love
and my mother said, Yes, that's the reason
I married your Dad in the loving season.

SATNAV

turn left

at the end of the road

       turn right

        turn right

after

  two hundred yards

      cross the roundabout

        second exit

cross the roundabout

(bloody recycling day just my luck
men in luminous coats nonchalant
calling across
waving me on
lorry gaping)

        after three hundred yards

     keep left

   keep left

KEEP LEFT

(mind the bike
no signals ever heard of signals?
dog alone school
woman with lead
and grim expression
kids with football careful careful)

                              ahead
bear left

bear left

(leafy
two children pram
mother bending
watch children have ball
lights green yes
late need green slow
slow thirty flashing)

 at the end of the road

                  go right on the roundabout

                                    fourth exit

(one two three raining a bit
good gardens need rain
no gardens here
pavement wet women in saris
one crying for some reason
 man moustache laughing in doorway café
cat crossing like Sufi
he died
get round this van
white van double parked
 bikes Bangladesh
had a driver traffic worse in Bangladesh
bikes worse
beggars worse too
bugger red lights maybe make it through

oh no OHNOONONONONONO)

turn around when possible

turn around when possible

turn around when possible

(impossible
too late
much too late)

At the end of the road

you have reached your destination

You have reached your destination

at the end of

the road you have

the road at the end of.

at the end of
the road.

at the end of
the road.

NAVIGATE TO
navigate to
navigate to
navigate to

SELECT YOUR DESTINATION

LOW ACHIEVER

He climbed to the foot of the tree.

And stood on his head with some glee.

When they called him a clown

He said "I can look down

Past my feet, on high flyers who look down on me."

FIGURATIVELY SPEAKING

Metaphors! she said. They're a closed book to me...
Similes? I need similes like I need a hole in the head!
No, I don't rejoice in noisy boys' voices
however fine the assonance – ssshhh!
Silence them sibilantly with alliteration.
Repetitions – can't swallow those....
they repeat on me....
and who needs rhetorical questions?

Rather unique tautology inspires me
to no onomatopoeic hoorays,
however much performance poets
huff and puff in purple passages.

And the pathetic fallacy is all wrong.
It's against nature. As for enjambment, it's

   such

   a
   waste
   of

space ......

and ellipses drive me dotty ....

no, figures of speech
are not to my taste, she said.

So... poetry's a bum steer up a blind alley then?
he responded.

   Eh? she said.

RETIREMENT PLANS

"When I grow old," said my mother, "I'll change my life.
I'll rent a garret on the Left Bank of the Seine
in Paris, give up being a mother and a wife,
spend my days painting, drink red wine all night,
 my friends will be artists - maybe I'll write."

"But what about Dad?" I objected.
My mother reflected.
"He'll be okay," she said.
"He'll buy a djellaba, sandals, a scarab
and live in the desert, along with the Arabs.
He's learning the lingo at evening class.
He'll go over to Gaza" – I thought, what a gas!

I'd spend April in Paris, winter with Dad –
there was going to be some fun to be had!
I hoped that my parents' dreams all would come true –
but after all that they just moved down to Bude.

GOAT BOOTS

Ants' sandals, wasps' socks
underpants for cockroaches
Don't you think that insects
should be clothed and not go nude?

Naked beetles long for berets,
lizards need their scarves.
Toads like smart tuxedos –
they don't do things by halves.

Goat boots, hippos' hats,
cardigans for cattle,
hats with corks for spiders
to attract the flies with rattles.

Gloves for gerbils, skirts for cats,
ball-dresses for tigers,
moccasins for micro-hogs and wellies
for fish swimming in the River Niger.

Don't you think it would be nice
to help God's little creatures
by making see-through macs for mice
and bras for the anteaters?

NON, SAID AUNTIE ANN

In This Country, But In Another Language, My Aunt Refuses To Marry The Men Everyone Wants Her To

Auntie Ann didn't want a man
Michel begged, "Please adore me,"
But "Non" said Auntie Ann.

She didn't want a man from Cannes;
then Carlo said, "Sposarmi?"
But Auntie Anne didn't want a man;

though Carlo was her ardent fan
from Naples warm and balmy,
"No, No!" said Auntie Ann.

And she had offers from Sudan
from very wealthy Swamis
but Auntie Ann didn't want a man

and told them so then turned and ran
and joined the Sally Army.
"No, No!" said Auntie Ann.

Michel and Carlo and the Swami
said that Auntie Ann was barmy
but Auntie Anne didn't want a man:
"Non" said Auntie Ann.

FAUX-PAS

Just when you thought it was safe to admit
that you never had been there or cared much for it,
just when you'd decided to really come clean
and tell them how totally bored you had been
just when you thought they had stopped up their ears
and no-one was watching and no-one would hear,
just then came the lull in the talk and you said
the words that made everyone wish you were dead.

GOD – THE PRESS CONFERENCE

What is the secret of my success?
Omnipotence helps, I guess.

Your competitors?

No, I don't want to comment on Lucifer Inc.,
though I read that our rivals are right in the pink.
A long time ago, the decision was made
and I guess they're still doing a pretty good trade.

Was the casting a problem?

Yes, the casting was difficult - field was quite small -
it was Adam or no-one set up for the Fall.
But Evie turned out to be rather a babe -
such a shame, that bad business later, with Abe.

Your son?
                You mean was he a chip off the old block?
Ask one of those chaps who likes wearing a frock.
He don't take after me - a lot more pacific -
and apart from his blockbuster, not so prolific.

And the future?

What am I working on in the next year?
Maybe tone down the pleasures, jack up the fear.

What would you have chosen to do differently?

..... Maybe called it a day when I'd created trees.

OK folks – no more questions today – busy schedule ...
[God has left the building .....)

A RECIPE FOR DISASTER (Serves 2)

Take an ounce of ground glass and two hearts

crushed in their own poison.

Blend with a spoonful of the blushful Hippocrene

(if unavailable, Tesco Sauvignon will do).

Season with hemlock, sand and thyme.

Set aside.

Add an addled egg, lightly beaten

until you can't hear its cries.

The mixture should not sweat.

Add the flower: rue or heartsease or

love-lies-a-bleeding should do, whatever is in season.

Transfer to a low heat and continue stirring

until the roux darkens and bubbles from below.

Add more wine, waters of the Lethe

or milk of human kindness if you can find it.

Pour into moulds and freeze.

This will keep for many years.

Serve partially defrosted,

heated or rehashed,

as a starter or a main dish

at any special family occasion.

ANIMAL PSYCHOLOGY

Wanderlust is not uncommon among hamsters
since they first perfected travelling on wheels.
Schadenfreude is a trait that some rabbits - one in eight -
will admit to, with vicious little squeals.

Claustrophobia's a problem for the ferret
because travelling in trousers makes them sick.
Hysteria is found in many moles underground
so they have to dig their tunnels very quick.

Glauckenstücke is what every goldfish feels
when it knows it has been revelling too much
in the sufferings of flatfish who've been bullied by catfish
or the battered cod the cat won't even touch.

Aphasia can be fatal for a parrot
Dyspraxia affects one snake in three
Guinea pigs who can't relax get mild panic attacks
but respond quite well to water therapy.

Start Living your Tomorrow from Today

(Thanks to Saga Magazine advertisements)

Cross your closest friends from your Christmas list
and write DEAD across their names.
Begin ordering all your food online
because you fear you may fall over
if you go shopping on foot.
If you do go out, take a stick with you,
to trip up younger walkers.
Get a state-of-the-art hearing aid.
Don't wear it. Ignore people if they speak quietly
and tell them not to shout if they speak loudly.
Fit a stair lift and ride up and down just for fun
(it's never been easier says Saga Magazine)
Wear a support stocking and/or a truss
whether you need it or not.
Take a new driving test.
Fail it by driving the wrong way on roundabouts.
Remind any young people you meet
that you've seen it all before.
Get a cat and overfeed it.
Ring radio shows to complain about
decimalization and the price of cat food.
Write poems about getting old.

IN THE CAFÉ DES ARTISTES

She was the Mona Lisa
but he was not Leonardo.
He was an action painting
and she was no Pollock.
Random accident had contrived to mark
the slack canvas of his face.

She was an Italian Arte Povera.
He offered to frame her in gold,
painted a glowing picture of life with
an old master. But with glazed eyes
she brushed him off and when

he offered to show her his etchings
she said she would stick to pork scratchings
in the Cafe Des Artistes.

Travelling

She was smirking in a convertible in Berlin,

he was frowning in a street-car in Saigon.

She was riding in a dog-cart in Tallinn,

he was trying to hail a taxi-cab in Bonn.

She was beaming on a bendy bus in Barcelona,

he was frowning in a transit van in Tring.

She was riding on a camel to Verona,

he was flying in an airship for a fling.

She was joking in a coach bound for Iran,

he was tearful in an Amazon canoe.

She was shouting on a moped in Milan,

he was snarling in a box-car in Peru.

She was singing on a swing in Madagascar,

He was weeping on a Chattanoga choo-choo

she was crooning to the moon in downtown Redcar.

He was train-spotting on platform number two.

she was sorry on a lorry by Loch Lomond;

he was smiling on a bicycle in Iceland,

She was waving on a roundabout at Drummond

he was cycling on a red trishaw in Ireland.

And when she saw him walking down the street

she hoped there was a chance that they would meet.

HAVE APE, WILL TRAVEL

Transportation of a monkey
on a first class ticket
is forbidden by Southern Railways.
I discovered this fact
when travelling in company
with my own Proboscis Monkey.
I'd dressed him carefully,
in robes and slippers,
but the inspector was not fooled,
though I noticed a group of gorillas
had slipped under his guard.

I noticed a group of gorillas

had slipped under his guard.

THE WORLD'S A STAGE

enter stage left
strut, weep, laugh, wear disguises
exit to applause

enter to applause
laugh weep avoid the trapdoors
exit unprompted

enter to applause
transformations, alarums
exit unscripted

whether pursued by a bear

or not.

This book is for the two people living
that I love most in the world.
They know who they are.

Guildford 2013